Microsoft Word 2013 Essentials

Michelle N. Halsey

ISBN-10: 1-64004-157-5

ISBN-13: 978-1-64004-157-8

Silver City Publications & Training, L.L.C.
P.O. Box 1914
Nampa, ID 83653
https://www.silvercitypublications.com/shop/

Contents

Chapter 1 – Opening Word

In this chapter, you will learn how to open Word, where you will first encounter the Recent list and other ways you can start a document. You will learn how to open files and how to create a blank document or a document from a template.

Opening Word

To open Word in Windows 8, use the following procedure.

Step 1: From the Start page, select the Word 2013 icon.

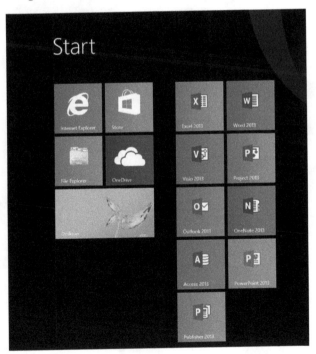

Use this procedure if using Windows 7or previous versions of Widows:

Step 1: Select the Start icon from the lower left side of the screen.

Step 2: Select **All Programs**.

Step 3: Select **Microsoft Office**.

Step 4: Select **Microsoft Office Word 2013**.

Using the Recent List

To open a document from the Recent list, use the following procedure.

Step 1: Select the document that you want to open from the Recent list.

To pin an item on the Recent list, use the following procedure.

Step 1: Click the pin on the right side of the Recent list item.

The item moves to the top section of the Recent list.

To unpin an item, click the pin on the right side of the Recent list again. The item returns to the previous location in the Recent list.

Opening Files

To open a document, use the following procedure.

Step 1: Select **Open Other Documents** from the bottom of the Recent list. Or select **Open** from the Backstage View.

Step 2: Select one of the **Places** you would like to look for the document. The default options are Recent Documents, your Microsoft SkyDrive location, and your Computer.

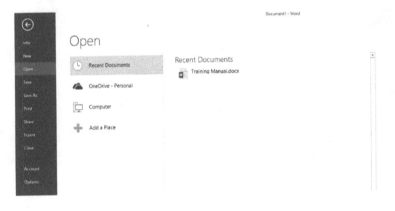

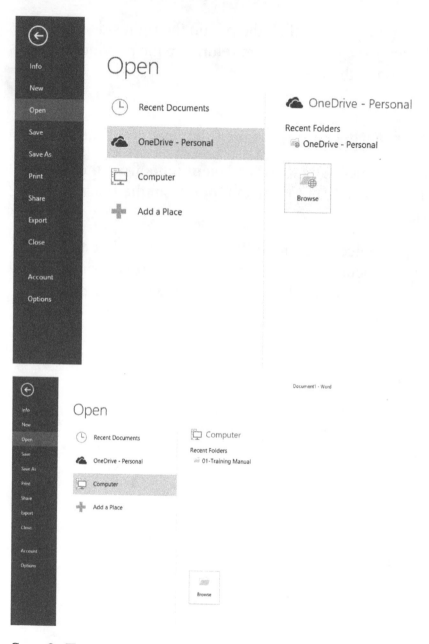

Step 3: To open a document from the SkyDrive or your computer, select **Browse**.

Step 4: In the *Open* dialog box, navigate to the location of the file you want to open. Select it and select **Open**.

Creating a Blank Document

To create a blank document, use the following procedure.

Step 1: If the Backstage view is not showing, select the **File** tab from the Ribbon. Select **New**.

Step 2: From the **New** tab, or if you have just opened Word 2013, select **Blank Document**.

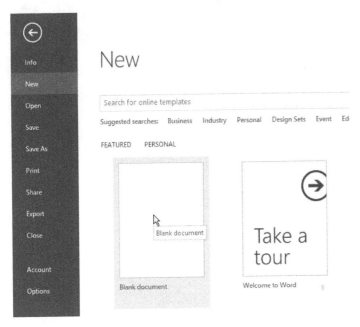

Creating a Document From a Template

To create a blank document from a template, use the following procedure.

Step 1: If the Backstage view is not showing, select the **File** tab from the Ribbon. Select **New**.

Step 2: From the **New** tab, or if you have just opened Word 2013, select the template you want to use.

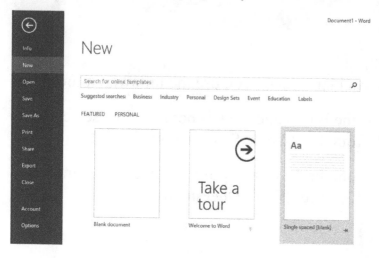

Step 3: Select **Create**.

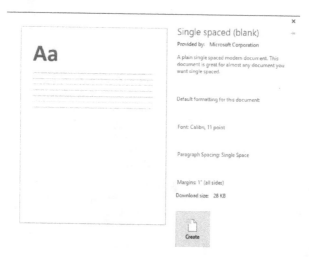

You can use the left and right arrows to review the other templates in the current search.

To search for a template and filter the results, use the following procedure.

Step 1: Select one of the Suggested Search terms or enter a term in the Search box and press Enter.

Step 2: To apply a filter, select the Filter term from the list on the right side of the screen.

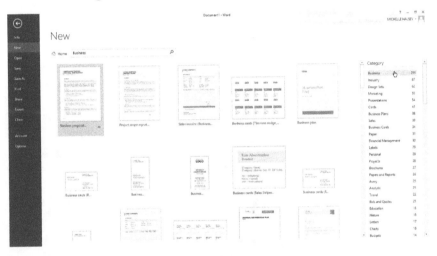

Step 3: To return to the list of templates, select **Home**.

Chapter 2 – Working with the Interface

In this chapter, we will introduce you to the Word 2013 interface, which uses the Ribbon from the previous two versions of Word. You will get a closer look at the Ribbon, as well as the Navigation pane and the Status bar. You will also learn how to manage your Microsoft account right from a new item above the Ribbon. This chapter introduces you to the Backstage view, where all of the functions related to your files live. You will learn how to save files. Finally, we will look at closing files and closing the application.

Understanding the Interface

The Word interface includes the Ribbon, the Navigation pane, the document window, the Quick Access toolbar, and the Status bar.

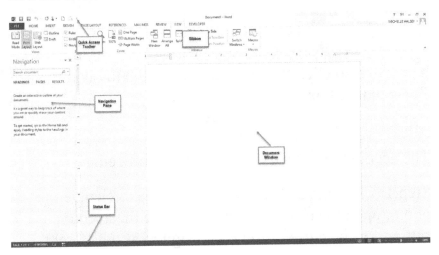

Each Tab in the Ribbon contains many tools for working with your document. To display a different set of commands, click the Tab name. Buttons are organized into groups according to their function.

The Quick Access toolbar appears at the top of the Word window. It provides you with one-click shortcuts to commonly used functions, like save, undo, and redo.

The Navigation pane allows you to quickly move through headings, pages, or search results.

The Status bar shows your current page, the word count, the language setting for proofing, and if any macros are currently running. It also allows you to quickly change your view or zoom of the document.

To zoom in or out, use the following procedure.

Step 1: Click the minus sign in the Status bar to zoom out. Click the plus sign in the Status bar to zoom in. You can also drag the slider to adjust the zoom.

You can also click the number percentage to open the *Zoom* dialog box.

About Your Account and Feedback

The account options use the following procedure.

Step 1: Click the arrow next to the name to change the photo, open the profile information, see the account setting for the current user, or to sign in as a different user.

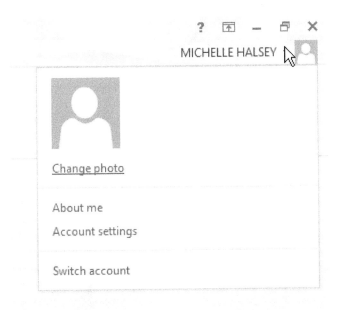

To send feedback to Microsoft, use the following procedure.

Step 1: Select the Smile icon at the top right corner of the screen.

Step 2: Select Send a Smile or Send a Frown.

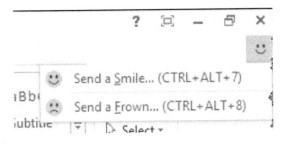

Step 3: Enter the information requested in the Microsoft Office Feedback dialog. Select **Send**.

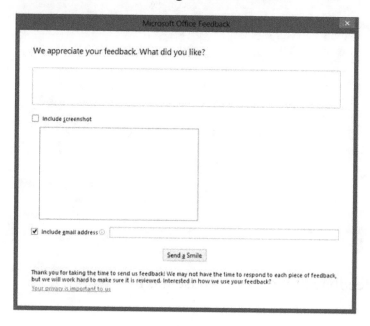

An Introduction to Backstage View

The Backstage View, use the following procedure.

Step 1: Select the **File** tab on the Ribbon.

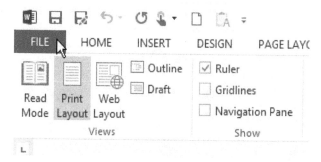

Word displays the Backstage View, open to the Info tab by default. A sample is illustrated below.

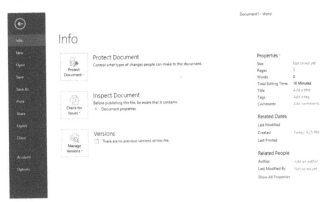

Saving Files

To save a document that has not been previously saved, use the following procedure.

Step 1: Select the **File** tab on the Ribbon.

Step 2: Select the **Save** command in the Backstage View.

Step 3: Select the **Place** where you want to save the document.

Step 4: If you choose your SkyDrive, you can select the **Documents** folder. If you choose your Computer, select your **Current Folder** or one of your **Recent Folders**. Or in either place, you can choose **Browse** to select a new location.

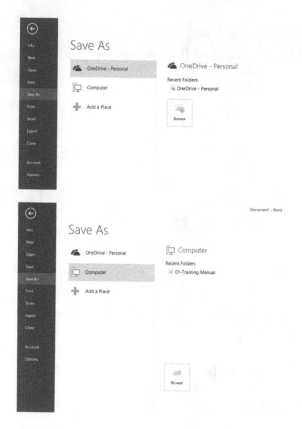

Step 5: The *Save As* dialog opens. Enter a **File Name**, and if desired, navigate to a new location to store the file. Select **Save**.

Closing Files vs. Closing Word

To close a file, use the following procedure.

Step 1: Select the **File** tab from the Ribbon.

Step 2: Select **Close** from The Backstage View.

If you have not saved your file, you will see the following message.

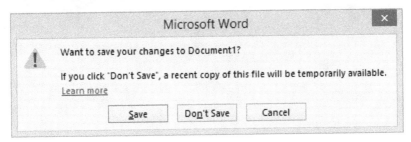

To close the application (if only one document is open), use the following procedure.

Step 1: Click the X at the top right corner of the window.

Chapter 3 – Your First Document

In this chapter, you will create your first document. You will learn how to type text and select it with a mouse or keyboard. With text selected, you can edit or delete text, or you can use the mouse to drag and drop text to a new location. You will also learn how to insert symbols and numbers. Finally, this chapter will cover how to start a new page.

Typing Text

The following diagram shows the cursor location in a blank document.

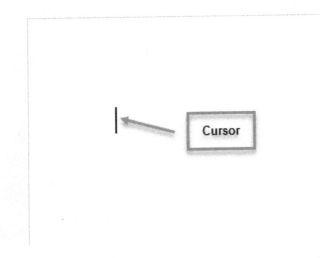

Sample text for students to type: The quick brown fox jumped over the lazy dog.

Selecting Text with the Mouse or Keyboard

To use the keyboard to select text, use the following procedure.

Step 1: Using the arrow keys, place the cursor either at the beginning of the text you want to select, or at the end of the text you want to select.

Step 2: Hold down the shift key while pressing the arrow key to select text in that direction.

The selected text is highlighted.

The quick brown fox jumped over the lazy dog.

To use the mouse to select text, use the following procedure.

Step 1: Point the mouse to either the beginning or the end of the text you want to select.

Step 2: Hold the left mouse button down.

Step 3: Move the mouse to select the text. You can move left, right, up and/or down.

Step 4: Let the mouse button up when you have finished selecting the text.

The mouse shortcuts for selecting text are:

- You can double click a word to select it.

- You can click three times on a paragraph to select the whole paragraph.

- You can click to the left of a line to select the whole line.

- You can press Shift while clicking to add to your selection. The selections must be next to each other.

- You can press Control while clicking to add non-congruent text to your selection.

The quick brown fox jumped over the lazy dog.

Editing and Deleting Text

- **Backspace key** – Deletes single or multiple characters backwards, or use to delete selected text

- **Delete key** – Deletes single or multiple characters forwards, or use to delete selected text

- **Insert** – Place cursor anywhere in text to begin typing. The original text moves to accommodate the inserted text.

- **Replace** – Select text and begin typing to replace the text.

Dragging and Dropping Text

To drag and drop selected text, use the following procedure.

Step 1: Select the text you want to move.

Step 2: Hold the left mouse pointer down.

Step 3: Move the cursor to the location where you want to move the text. The cursor has an arrow and a small box to indicate that you are moving text.

The quick brown fox jumped over the lazy dog.

Step 4: Let the mouse button go when the cursor is in the desired location.

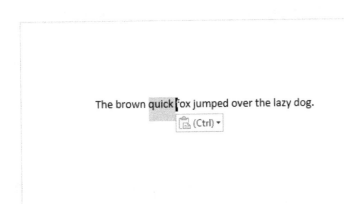

The text remains highlighted in case you want to move it again or continue editing it.

Inserting a Symbol or Number

To insert a symbol, use the following procedure.

Step 1: Select the **Insert** tab from the Ribbon.

Step 2: Select **Symbol**.

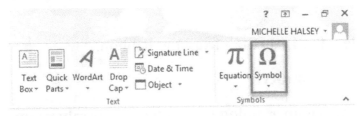

Step 3: Select the symbol from the list, if it is shown. If not, select **More Symbols**.

Step 4: In the *Symbols* dialog box, select an option from the **Font** drop down list and the **Subset** drop down list to navigate through the available symbols. You can also use the scroll bar on the right. Select the symbol you want and select **Insert**.

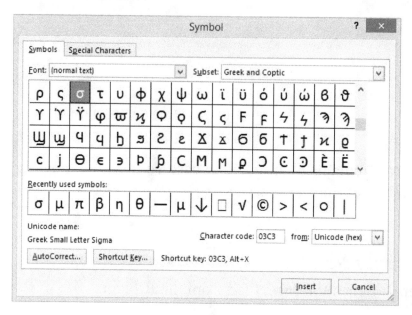

To insert a specially formatted number, use the following procedure.

Step 1: Select the **Insert** tab from the Ribbon.

Step 2: Select **Number**.

Step 3: In the *Number* dialog box, enter the **Number** you want to format.

Step 4: Select the **Number type** from the list.

Step 5: Select **OK**.

Starting a New Page

To insert a page break, use the following procedure.

Step 1: Press Enter to start a new paragraph. This will be important for formatting the document later.

Step 2: Select the **Page Layout** Tab on the Ribbon.

Step 3: Select the **Breaks** tool on the Page Setup Group.

Step 4: Select **Page**.

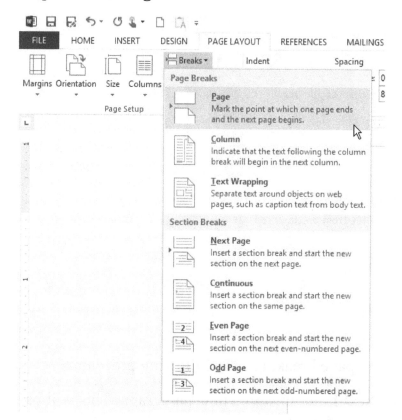

Chapter 4 – Basic Editing Tasks

The Word 2013 editing tools make editing your document a breeze. This chapter covers how to cut, copy and paste text, as well as how to undo and redo tasks. It explains how to find and replace text, such as when you want to change a word or phrase throughout your document. It introduces the Word Options dialog box to set default paste options. Finally, it explains how to check your spelling.

Using Cut, Copy, and Paste

To cut and paste text, use the following procedure.

Step 1: Highlight the text you want to cut.

Step 2: Right click the mouse to display the context menu and select cut.

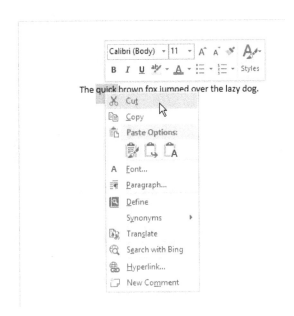

Step 3: Move the cursor to the new location.

Step 4: Right click the mouse to display the context menu and select the Text Only paste option, as illustrated below. Note that the context menu dims so that you can see a preview of your work.

To copy and paste text using the keyboard shortcuts, use the following procedure:

Step 1: Highlight the text you want to cut and press the Control key and the C key at the same time.

Step 2: Move the cursor to the new location.

Step 3: Press the Control key and the V key at the same time.

Using Undo and Redo

To undo their most recent typing or command, use the following procedure.

Step 1: Select the Undo command from the Quick Access Toolbar.

To redo the last command or repeat it, use the following procedure.

Step 1: Select the Redo command from the Quick Access Toolbar.

Finding and Replacing Text

To find and replace one instance at a time of "Customer Name" in the sample document, use the following procedure.

Step 1: Select **Replace** from the Editing group on the **Home** tab of the Ribbon.

Step 2: In the *Find and Replace* dialog box, enter the exact text you want to find in the **Find what** field.

Step 3: Enter the replacement text in the **Replace with** field.

Step 4: Select **Find next** to find the next instance of the item.

Step 5: When Word highlights the item, select **Replace** to delete the "find" item and paste the "replace" item.

Step 6: Select **Close** when you have finished. Or select **Cancel** to close the dialog box without making any replacements.

To Replace all instances of an item, use the following procedure.

Step 1: Open the Find and Replace dialog box by selecting **Replace** from the Ribbon.

Step 2: Enter the exact text you want to find in the **Find what** field.

Step 3: Enter the replacement text in the **Replace with** field.

Step 4: Select **Replace All**.

Step 5: Select **Close** when you have finished. Or select **Cancel** to close the dialog box without making any replacements.

Word replaces all instances of the item. If your cursor was not at the beginning of the document, or if you have text selected, Word asks if you want to continue searching at the beginning. When finished, Word displays a message indicating how many replacements were made.

Setting Paste Options

To open the Word Options dialog box for pasting options, use the following procedure.

Step 1: Select the **Paste** command from the Clipboard group of the **Home** tab on the Ribbon.

Step 2: Select the **Set Default Paste** option.

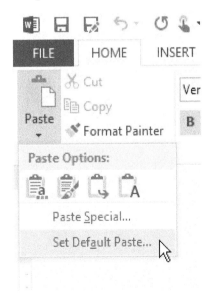

The cut, copy, and paste options on the *Word Options* dialog box.

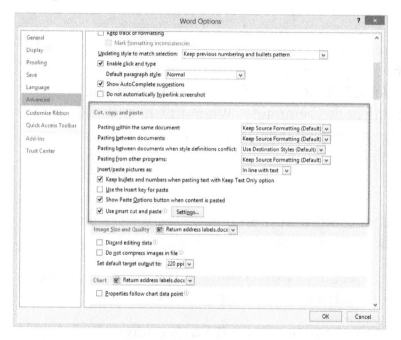

Checking Your Spelling

The following diagram shows the context menu for a misspelled word. The following example uses a misspelling of the word "information."

Step 1: Right click a misspelled word to display the context menu.

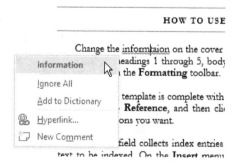

To open the Spelling pane, use the following procedure.

Step 1: Select **Spelling** from the **Proofing** group on the **Review** tab of the Ribbon.

Discuss the buttons on the Spelling pane.

- The **Ignore** button allows you to keep the word as the current spelling, but only for the current location.

- The **Ignore All** button allows you to ignore the misspelling for the whole document.

- The **Add** button allows you to add the word to your dictionary for all Word documents.

37

- The Suggestions area lists possible changes for the misspelling. There may be many choices, just one, or no choices, based on Word's ability to match the error to other possibilities.

- The **Change** button allows you to change the misspelled word to the highlighted choice in the Suggestions area. You can highlight any word in the Suggestions area and select Change.

- The **Change All** button allows you to notify Word to make this spelling correction any time it encounters this spelling error in this document.

Chapter 5 – Basic Formatting Tasks

Word 2013 allows you to enhance your text in many ways. In this chapter, we will discuss the different types of formatting, as well as cover the most basic types of formatting your words. This includes the font face, size, and color, as well as highlighting and enhancing the text.

Understanding Levels of Formatting

The Font and Paragraph groups on the Home tab of the Ribbon.

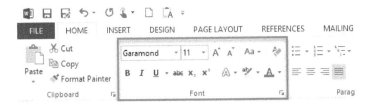

Changing Font Face and Size

To change the font face and size using the Ribbon tools, use the following procedure.

Step 1: Select the text you want to change.

Step 2: Select the arrow next to the current font name to display the list of available fonts.

Step 3: Use the scroll bar or the down arrow to scroll down the list of fonts.

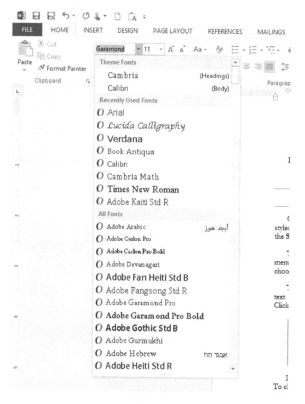

Step 4: Select the desired font to change the font of text.

Step 5: With the text still selected, select the arrow next to the current font size to see a list of common font sizes.

Step 6: Use the scroll bar or the down arrow key to scroll to the size you want and select it. You can also highlight the current font size and type in a new number to indicate the font size you want.

The font context list that appears when you select text, use the following procedure.

Step 1: Select the text you want to change.

Step 2: A very faint context menu appears. Move your mouse over the menu to make sure it stays visible. If you do not see it, you can always right-click the mouse to make it appear.

Step 3: Select the new font face or font size just as you would on the Ribbon.

Changing the Font Color

To select a color for their fonts from the gallery, use the following procedure.

Step 1: Select the text you want to change.

Step 2: Select the arrow next to the Font Color tool on the Ribbon to display the gallery. Or select the same tool from the context menu (appears when you select text or by right-clicking).

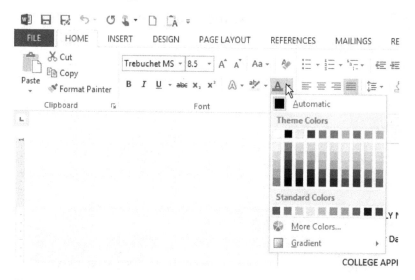

Step 3: Select the color to change the font color.

Use the following procedure to change the Colors of the text.

Step 1: Select the text you want to change.

Step 2: Select the arrow next to the Font Color tool on the Ribbon to display the gallery. Or select the same tool from the context menu (appears when you select text or by right-clicking).

Step 3: Select **More Colors** to open the Colors dialog box.

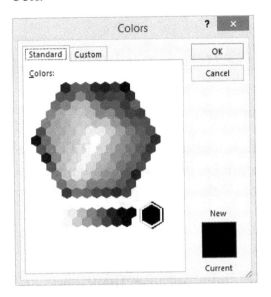

In the *Standard Colors* dialog box, simply click the color and select **OK** to use that color.

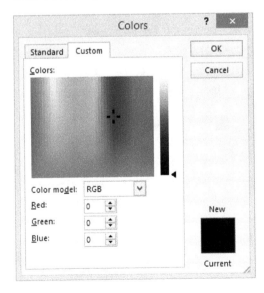

In the *Custom Colors* dialog box, you can click the color, or you can enter the red, green, and blue values to get a

43

precise color. When you have the color you want, select **OK**.

Highlighting Text

To highlight text they have already selected, use the following procedure.

Step 1: Select the text you want to highlight.

Step 2: Select the Text Highlight tool from the Ribbon or the formatting context menu. Or select the arrow next to the Text Highlighting tool to choose a highlighting color.

To turn on the highlighting tool to highlight different areas of text, use the following procedure.

Step1: Select the Text Highlight tool from the Ribbon or the formatting context menu. Or select the arrow next to the Text Highlighting tool to choose a highlighting color.

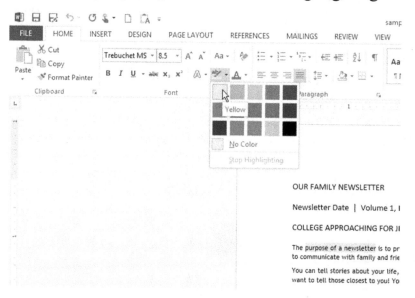

The cursor changes to a highlighting cursor, as illustrated below.

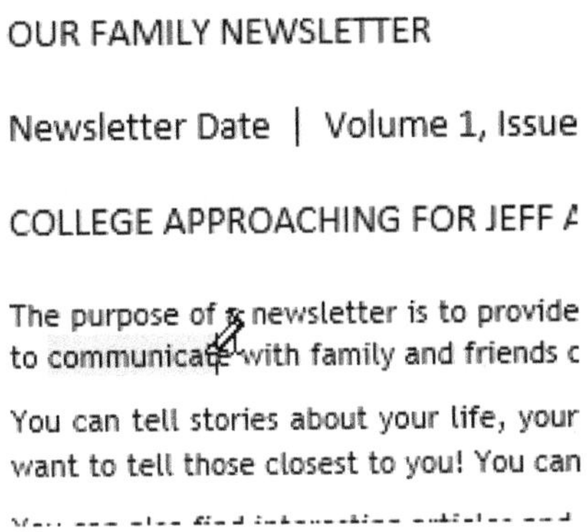

OUR FAMILY NEWSLETTER

Newsletter Date | Volume 1, Issue

COLLEGE APPROACHING FOR JEFF /

The purpose of ᵃ newsletter is to provide
to communicate with family and friends c

You can tell stories about your life, your
want to tell those closest to you! You can

Step 2: Select the text you want to highlight. Word will continue highlighting as many different unconnected pieces of text as you like.

Step 3: To stop highlighting, select the Text Highlight tool again and choose Stop Highlighting. Or just click the Text Highlight tool again.

Adding Font Enhancements
The tools used to add font enhancements.

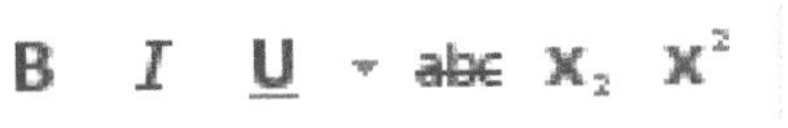

B *I* <u>U</u> ▾ a̶b̶c̶ X_2 X^2

- Bold
- Italic
- Underline
- Strikethrough
- Subscript

- Superscript

Clearing Formatting

To use the clear formatting tool, use the following procedure:

Step 1: Select the text that has been formatted with the formatting properties that you want to remove.

Step 2: Select the Clear Formatting tool.

Chapter 6 –Formatting Paragraphs

Paragraph formatting controls the look and feel of an entire paragraph. In this chapter, we will discuss how to change the spacing of your text, both the line spacing and the space in between paragraphs. We will also address setting the alignment and using tabs and indents. We will also practice using bullets and numbering the document and learn how to add borders and shading to the text. Finally, we will take a look at the Paragraph dialog, where you can format many aspects of your paragraph at once.

Changing Spacing

To adjust the line spacing using the Line Spacing tool on the Ribbon, use the following procedure.

Step 1: With your cursor anywhere in the paragraph you want to adjust (the text does not have to be selected), select the Line and Paragraph spacing tool from the Ribbon.

Step 2: Select one of the following options:

- 1.0 – single spacing

- 1.15 – provides a little more space than single spacing

- 1.50 – One and a half line spacing

- 2.0 – double spacing

- 2.5 – two and a half line spacing

- 3.0 – triple spacing

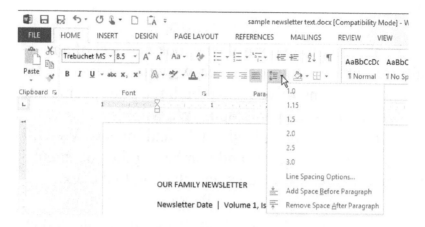

To add or remove space before or after a paragraph, use the following procedure.

Step 3: With your cursor anywhere in the paragraph you want to adjust (the text does not have to be selected), select the Line and Paragraph spacing tool from the Ribbon.

Step 4: The Paragraph spacing options listed are based on your current settings. You can choose one of the following to add or remove space before or after your paragraph:

- Add Space Before Paragraph

- Remove Space Before Paragraph

- Add Space After Paragraph

- Remove Space After Paragraph

The amount added by default is usually 12 points. To add more, you will need to use the Paragraph dialog box.

Setting the Alignment

To adjust the alignment for the paragraph, use the following procedure.

Step 1: With your cursor anywhere in the paragraph you want to adjust (the text does not have to be selected), select the desired alignment tool from the Ribbon. You can also select multiple paragraphs by selecting the text.

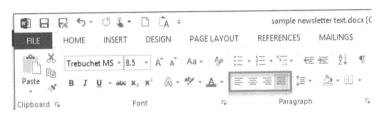

Using Indents and Tabs

To add a whole paragraph indent, use the following procedure.

Step 1: With your cursor anywhere in the paragraph you want to adjust (the text does not have to be selected), select the Indent tool from the Ribbon. You can also select multiple paragraphs by selecting the text.

Adding Bullets and Numbering

To create a simple bulleted or numbered list, use the following procedure.

Step 1: Select the paragraphs you want to turn into a bulleted or numbered list.

Step 2: Select the Bullets or Numbering tool from the Ribbon.

The Bullet Library and the Numbering Library.

Step 1: Select the arrow next to the Bullets tool or the Numbering tool on the Ribbon to view the library options.

Step 2: Select an option to create a list with that option.

To open the Define New Bullet dialog box, the Define New Numbering Format dialog box, and the Set Numbering Value dialog box, use the following procedure.

Step 1: Select the arrow next to the Bullets tool or the Numbering tool on the Ribbon.

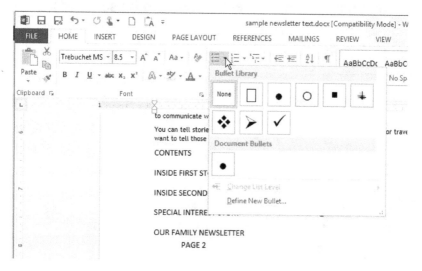

Step 2: Select the Define New Bullet option, the Define New Number Format, or the Set Numbering Value option from the menu.

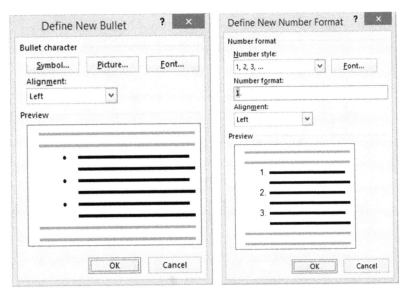

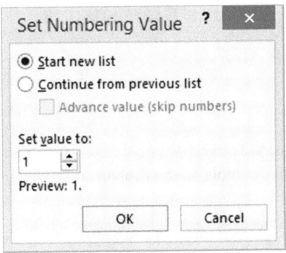

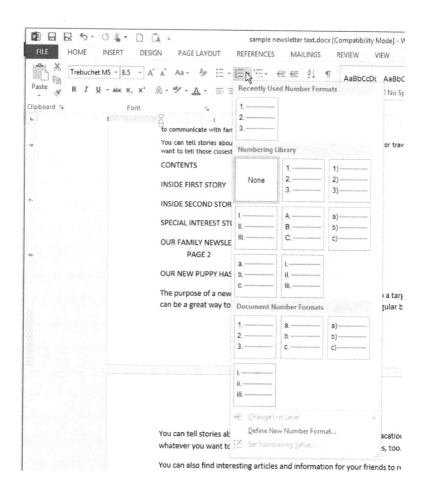

Adding Borders and Shading

The Shading and Border tools on the Ribbon are illustrated below.

To add shading to selected paragraphs, use the following procedure.

Step 1: Select the paragraphs you want to shade. If you only want to shade one paragraph, your cursor can be anywhere in the paragraph without selecting it.

Step 2: Select the color from the Shading tool on the Ribbon. The Shading tool includes the same gallery of colors as previously introduced.

To add borders to selected paragraphs, use the following procedure.

Step 1: Select the paragraphs you want to border. If you only want to put borders on one paragraph, your cursor can be anywhere in the paragraph without selecting it.

Step 2: Select the border you want to use from the Borders tool on the Ribbon. The Borders tool includes several options for borders. Some of the options only apply for tables.

The Borders and Shading dialog box.

Step 1: Open the Borders and Shading dialog box by selecting Borders and Shading from the Borders tool on the Ribbon.

The Borders tab of the Borders and Shading dialog box is illustrated below.

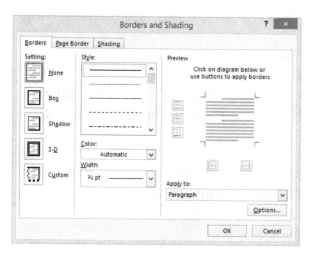

The Shading tab of the Borders and Shading dialog box is illustrated below.

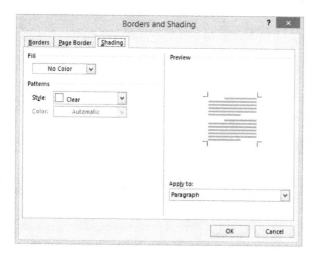

Chapter 7 – Advanced Formatting Tasks

This chapter introduces some of the more advanced formatting tasks for formatting your text in Word 2013. This chapter covers changing the case (capitalization) of words. You will also learn to use the format painter, to quickly format words to match others. This chapter introduces the Font dialog box for formatting several properties of your font at once. Finally, you will learn how to clear your formatting choices if you change your mind about the formatting.

Changing Case

To change the case, use the following procedure.

Step 1: Select the text you want to change.

Step 2: Select the Case tool from the **Font** group of the **Home** tab on the Ribbon.

Step 3: Select the Case option from the drop down list.

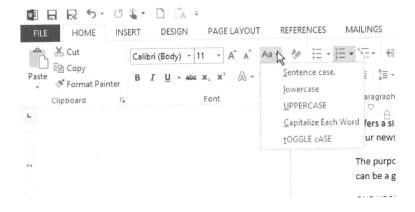

Using the Format Painter

To use the Format Painter, use the following procedure.

Step 1: Select the text that has been formatted with the formatting properties that you want to copy.

Step 2: Select the Format Painter tool.

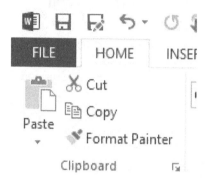

The cursor changes to a Format Painter cursor, as illustrated below.

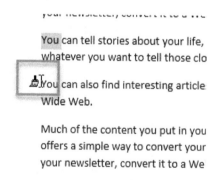

Step1: Select the text you want to format with the same properties.

The cursor returns to normal after applying the formatting properties once. You can always repeat the process to format more text with the same properties.

If you double-click the format painter tool before applying it to text, you can use it several times in a row. Just click the format painter tool when you are finished.

Creating Multilevel Lists

To create a multilevel list, use the following procedure.

Step 1: Select the Multilevel list tool from the Home tab on the Ribbon.

Step 2: Select the type of list that you would like to use from the gallery.

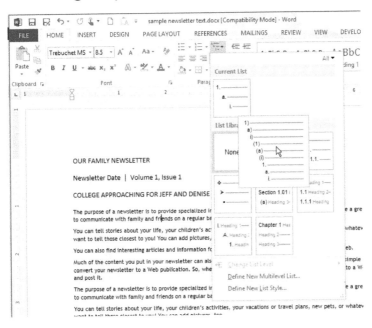

Step 3: Begin typing the list. In this example, you can use simple text, like "level 1" and "level 2".

Step 4: Press Enter to move to the next item.

Step 5: If the item is not automatically formatted/numbered properly, select **Change List Level** from the Multilevel list drop down list.

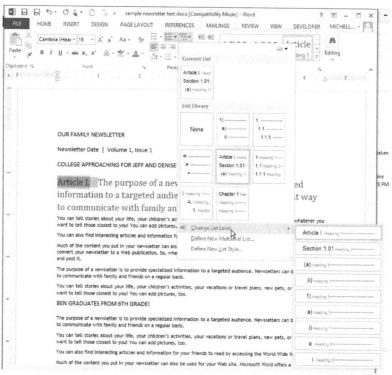

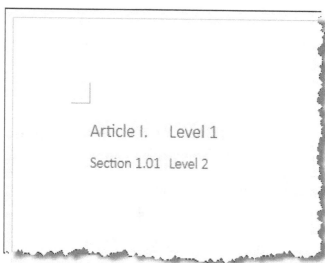

Using the Font Dialog

To open the Font dialog box, use the following procedure.

Step 1: Select the text you want to format.

Step 2: Select the square at the bottom right corner of the Font group in the Ribbon.

The following diagrams show the Font dialog box.

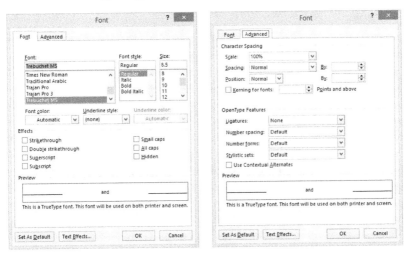

The following diagram shows the Set as Default dialog box.

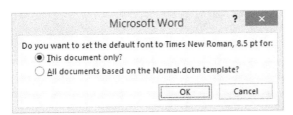

Review the Text Effects dialog box options. Click the icons at the top or the arrows to expand the available options for each item.

Using the Paragraph Dialog

Use the following procedure to use the Paragraph dialog box:

Step 1: With your cursor anywhere in the paragraph you want to adjust (the text does not have to be selected), select the Line and Paragraph spacing tool from the Ribbon.

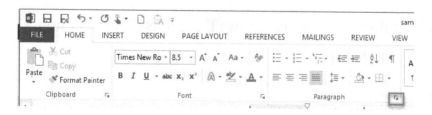

Step 2: Select the square at the bottom right corner of the Paragraph group in the Ribbon.

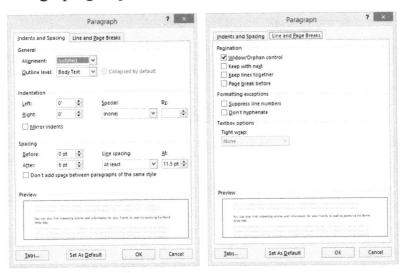

- The Special field allows you to select a first line only or hanging indent. Enter the measurement for the special indent in the **By** field. Check the **Mirror indents** to have the indent on both the left margin and the right margin by the same amounts.

- You can use the up and down arrows to adjust the indentation and spacing options. The arrows adjust the points in typographical increments. You can also enter any number to adjust the spacing more precisely.

- The Line Spacing field allows you to select from several line spacing options. If you select **At Least**, **Exactly**, or **Multiple**, enter the measurement (points or lines) in the **At** field.

- You can preview you selections at the bottom of the dialog box.

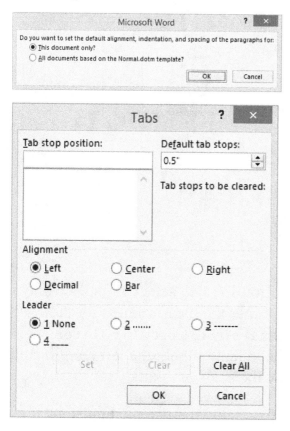

Chapter 8 – Working with Styles

Styles are a powerful formatting tool to take your Word 2013 document to the next level. Styles help provide consistency. They are also useful if you want to use certain advanced features like generated tables of contents. This chapter introduces styles and themes to help make your documents look great.

About Styles

The implications of using styles may not be apparent in shorter documents, but they are a great time saver for longer documents. They also help ensure that your document is consistently formatted. Styles also provide an easy way to easily change the look of the whole document if styles have been applied appropriately.

Once you have applied Heading styles to your document, the Navigation pane will also help you to quickly access different parts of the document based on the heading styles. Styles are a great time saver!

Applying a Style

Use the Style gallery to apply a paragraph or character style.

Step 1: Select the text you want to format, or simply place your cursor in the word or paragraph you want to format.

Step 2: Open the Style Gallery by clicking the down arrow next to the styles shown in the Styles group.

Step 3: Select the desired style to apply it to the current word or paragraph.

The Apply Styles dialog box.

Step 1: Select the text you want to format, or simply place your cursor in the word or paragraph you want to format.

Step 2: Open the Apply Styles dialog box by clicking the down arrow next to the styles shown in the Styles group, and selecting **Apply Styles** from the menu.

Step 3: To apply a style using the Apply Styles dialog box, simply begin typing the name of the style and press Enter when the desired style is displayed. Or use the drop down list to select the style.

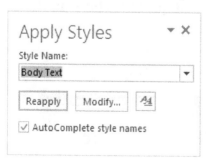

Changing the Theme

To change the theme, use the following procedure.

Step 1: Select the **Design** tab on the Ribbon.

Step 2: Select the **Themes** tool from the Ribbon to see the options.

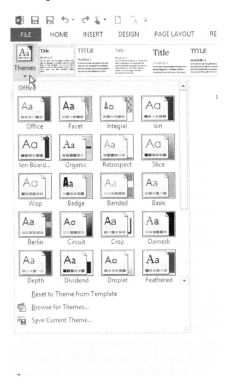

Step 3: Select a Theme from the list.

Changing the Style Set

To change the style set, use the following procedure.

Step 1: Select the **Design** tab on the Ribbon.

Step 2: Select the new style from the Document Formatting group.

Changing Theme Colors and Fonts

To change the theme colors or fonts, use the following procedure.

Step 1: Select the **Design** tab on the Ribbon.

Step 2: Select the **Colors** tool or the **Fonts** tool from the Ribbon to see the options.

Step 3: Select an option from the menu to change the color set or font set for the document.

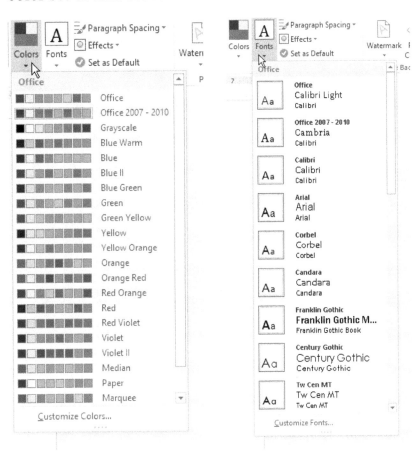

Chapter 9 – Formatting the Page

You have your text and paragraphs looking great, but what about the page? This chapter covers the basics of page formatting. You will learn how to format text into columns, how to change the orientation from portrait to landscape, how to add a page color or border, and how to add headers and footers.

Formatting Text as Columns

To create columns, use the following procedure.

Step 1: Select the **Page Layout** tab from the Ribbon.

Step 2: Select the **Columns** tool.

Step 3: Select the number or layout of columns that you want to use.

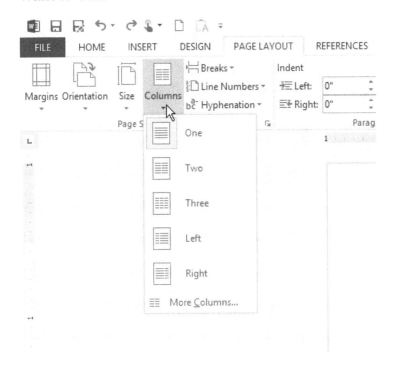

The *Columns* dialog box.

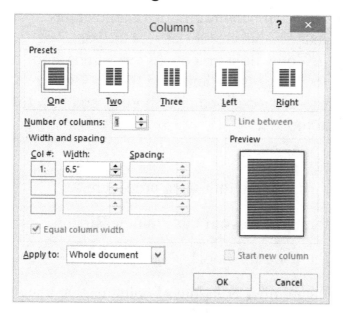

Changing Page Orientation

To change the page orientation, use the following procedure.

Step 1: Select the **Page Layout** tab from the Ribbon.

Step 2: Select **Orientation**.

Step 3: Select the orientation you want to use.

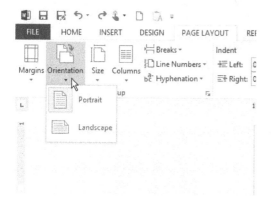

Changing the Page Color

To add color to the page, use the following procedure.

Step 1: Select the **Design** tab from the Ribbon.

Step 2: Select the **Page Colors** tool.

Step 3: Select a color from the gallery.

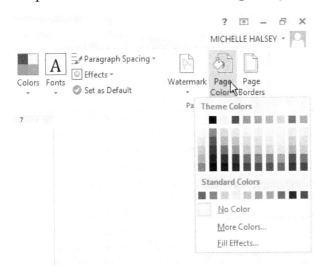

The *Fill Effects* dialog box.

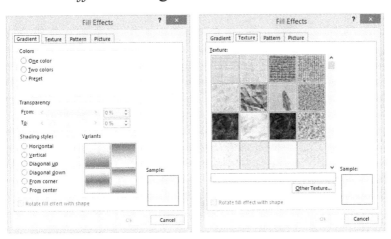

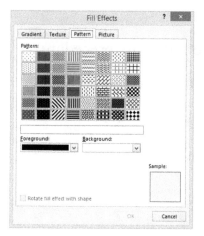
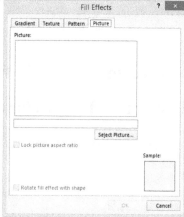

Adding a Page Border

To add a page border, use the following procedure.

Step 1: Select the **Design** tab from the Ribbon.

Step 2: Select **Page Borders**.

Step 3: Select the type of border using the **Setting** or **Style** options. You can select a color, the width, and even art. Click the diagram to create a custom border.

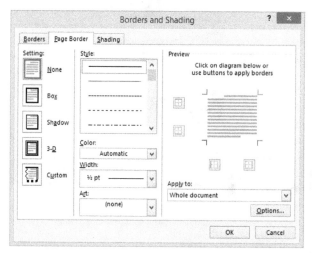

Adding Headers and Footers

To insert a header, use the following procedure.

Step 1: Select the **Insert** tab from the Ribbon.

Step 2: Select **Header**.

Step 3: Select the type of header that you want to use from the gallery.

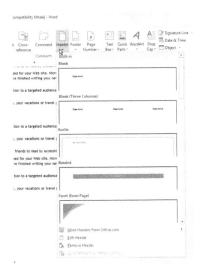

The following diagram shows the Header & Footer Tools Design tab.

Chapter 10 – Sharing Your Document

Now that your document is ready, it is time to share it! First, you will learn how to preview and print your document. When you have saved your document to the cloud, you can invite people, which sends a link so that you can share the document. You can also get a link to share the people, which send groups of people (such as when you do not know everyone's email address). Finally, you will learn how to email the document.

Previewing and Printing Your Document

To open the Print tab of the Backstage View to preview the document, use the following procedure.

Step 1: Select the **File** tab on the Ribbon.

Step 2: Select the **Print** tab in the Backstage View.

Discuss the buttons on the **Print** tab of the Backstage View.

- The **Print** button allows you to print the document using the current settings.

- The **Copies** field allows you to print one or more copies of the document.

- The **Printer** allows you to select a different printer. The printer properties link allows you to set the properties for that printer.

- The **Settings** tool allows you to select different pages of your document. You can even print document properties, such as a list of styles used in the document.

- The **pages** field allows you to specify a custom page range to print.

- The other **settings** control additional settings for print, such as one or two sided printing, whether multiple copies are collated, the orientation, the paper size, the default page margins, and how many pages to print per page.

- There is also a link to the **Page Setup** dialog box.

Sharing Your Document

To invite people to the document, use the following procedure.

Step 1: Select the **File** tab from the Ribbon to open the Backstage view.

Step 2: Select the **Share** tab.

Step 3: Select **Invite People**.

Step 4: Enter the names or email addresses for the people that you want to invite.

Step 5: Enter a message to include with the invitation.

Step 6: If desired, check the require user to sign-in before accessing document box to enhance the security of your document.

Step 7: Select **Share**.

To get a link for the document, use the following procedure.

Step 1: Select the **File** tab from the Ribbon to open the Backstage view.

Step 2: Select the **Share** tab.

Step 3: Select Get a Link.

Step 4: Select the **Create Link** button next to **View Link** or **Edit Link** (or both), depending on what type of editing rights you want to provide. You can copy the link and paste it to another location, such as an email or a blog page.

Step 5: If you want to remove the sharing rights, select **Disable Link**.

E-Mailing Your Document

To email an attachment or send a link, use the following procedure.

Step 1: Select the **File** tab on the Ribbon.

Step 2: Select the **Share** tab in the Backstage View.

Step 3: Select **Email**.

Step 4: Select **Send as Attachment** or **Send a Link**.

Step 5: Outlook opens with an email started.

- If you select **Send as Attachment**, the name of the document is used as the subject and the document is already attached to the email. Enter the email addresses and any personal message you want to include.

- If you select **Send a Link**, the name of the document is used as the subject and the link is included in the body message of the email. Enter the email addresses and any personal message that you want to include.

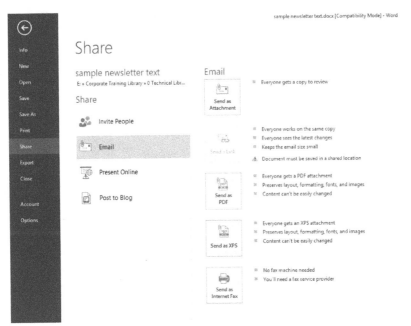

Additional Titles

The Technical Skill Builder series of books covers a variety of technical application skills. For the availability of titles please see https://www.silvercitypublications.com/shop/. Note the Master Class volume contains the Essentials, Advanced, and Expert (when available) editions.

Current Titles

Microsoft Excel 2013 Essentials

Microsoft Excel 2013 Advanced

Microsoft Excel 2013 Expert

Microsoft Excel 2013 Master Class

Microsoft Word 2013 Essentials

Microsoft Word 2013 Advanced

Microsoft Word 2013 Expert

Microsoft Word 2013 Master Class

Microsoft Project 2010 Essentials

Microsoft Project 2010 Advanced

Microsoft Project 2010 Expert

Microsoft Project 2010 Master Class

Microsoft Visio 2010 Essentials

Microsoft Visio 2010 Advanced

Microsoft Visio 2010 Master Class

Coming Soon

Microsoft Access 2013 Essentials

Microsoft Access 2013 Advanced

Microsoft Access 2013 Expert

Microsoft Access 2013 Master Class

Microsoft PowerPoint 2013 Essentials

Microsoft PowerPoint 2013 Advanced

Microsoft PowerPoint 2013 Expert

Microsoft PowerPoint 2013 Master Class

Microsoft Outlook 2013 Essentials

Microsoft Outlook 2013 Advanced

Microsoft Outlook 2013 Expert

Microsoft Outlook 2013 Master Class

Microsoft Publisher 2013 Essentials

Microsoft Publisher 2013 Advanced

Microsoft Publisher 2013 Master Class

Windows 7 Essentials

Windows 8 Essentials